L134

Design of plant, equipment and workplaces

Dangerous Substances and
Explosive Atmospheres Regulations 2002

APPROVED CODE OF PRACTICE
AND GUIDANCE

HSE BOOKS

© *Crown copyright 2003*

First published 2003

ISBN 0 7176 2199 5

All rights reserved. No part of this publication may be reproduced, stored in a retrieval system, or transmitted in any form or by any means (electronic, mechanical, photocopying, recording or otherwise) without the prior written permission of the copyright owner.

Applications for reproduction should be made in writing to:
Licensing Division, Her Majesty's Stationery Office,
St Clements House, 2-16 Colegate, Norwich NR3 1BQ
or by e-mail to hmsolicensing@cabinet-office.x.gsi.gov.uk

This Code has been approved by the Health and Safety Commission, with the consent of the Secretary of State. It gives practical advice on how to comply with the law. If you follow the advice you will be doing enough to comply with the law in respect of those specific matters on which the Code gives advice. You may use alternative methods to those set out in the Code in order to comply with the law.

However, the Code has special legal status. If you are prosecuted for breach of health and safety law, and it is proved that you did not follow the relevant provisions of the Code, you will need to show that you have complied with the law in some other way or a court will find you at fault.

The Regulations and Approved Code of Practice (ACOP) are accompanied by guidance which does not form part of the ACOP. Following the guidance is not compulsory and you are free to take other action. But if you do follow the guidance you will normally be doing enough to comply with the law. Health and safety inspectors seek to secure compliance with the law and may refer to this guidance as illustrating good practice.

Contents

Preface *iv*

Notice of Approval *v*

Introduction *1*

Regulation 5 - Assessment of the risks *3*
Risk assessment *3*
Changing processes and equipment *3*

Regulation 6 (and Schedule 1) - Elimination or reduction of risks from dangerous substances *4*
General principles on the selection of equipment, etc where dangerous substances are present *6*
Control measures *9*
Mitigation measures *14*
Other issues to consider on the control and mitigation of risks *16*
Making redundant plant and equipment safe *17*

References and further reading *19*

Preface

This publication contains an extract from the Dangerous Substances and Explosive Atmospheres Regulations[1] (regulations 5 and 6 and Schedule 1), together with an Approved Code of Practice and supporting guidance.

For convenience, the text of the Regulations is set out in *italic* type, with the ACOP in **bold** type and the accompanying guidance in normal type.

Notice of Approval

By virtue of section 16(1) of the Health and Safety at Work etc Act 1974 and with the consent of the Secretary of State for Work and Pensions, the Health and Safety Commission has on 8 April 2003 approved the Code of Practice entitled *Design of plant, equipment and workplaces*.

The Code of Practice gives practical guidance with respect to regulations 5 and 6 of the Dangerous Substances and Explosive Atmospheres Regulations 2002 with regard to the design of plant, equipment and workplaces that handles or processes dangerous substances.

The Code of Practice comes into effect on 27 October 2003.

Signed

MARK DEMPSEY
Secretary to the Health and Safety Commission
3 October 2003

Introduction

1 The Dangerous Substances and Explosive Atmospheres Regulations 2002[1] (DSEAR) are concerned with protection against risks from fire, explosion and similar events arising from dangerous substances used or present in the workplace. They set minimum requirements for the protection of workers from fire and explosion risks related to dangerous substances and potentially explosive atmospheres. The Regulations apply to employers and the self-employed at most workplaces in Great Britain where a dangerous substance is present or could be present.

2 DSEAR revokes, repeals or modifies a large amount of old legislation relating to flammable substances and dusts. Safety standards will be maintained through a combination of the requirements of DSEAR and Approved Codes of Practice (ACOPs) reflecting good practices in the old legislation.[2-6]

3 The key requirements in DSEAR are that risks from dangerous substances are assessed and eliminated or reduced. This ACOP provides practical advice on what employers need to do to meet the requirements of regulations 5 and 6 of DSEAR (on assessment and control of risks) prior to using any plant, equipment or area which handles, produces or processes dangerous substances, or making modifications, or changing the operating conditions or type of dangerous substance handled. This includes measures that may be needed to make redundant plant and equipment safe.

4 This publication is part of a series intended to support DSEAR. Other activity-related ACOPs and guidance material is available in the following publications:

(a) *Dangerous substances and explosive atmospheres*[2] - This provides an overview of how employers can meet their duties under DSEAR.

(b) *Storage of dangerous substances*[3] - This gives practical advice on the requirements of regulations 5 and 6 to assess the risks from, and the control and mitigation measures for, places where dangerous substances are stored. It includes the safe disposal of waste materials.

(c) *Control and mitigation measures*[4] - This gives practical advice on the requirements of regulations 5 and 6 to identify the hazards arising from the dangerous substance and put in place adequate ventilation, ignition control and separation measures to control risks.

(d) *Safe maintenance, repair and cleaning*[5] - This gives practical advice on identifying hazards and implementing appropriate control measures and systems of work during maintenance and other similar non-routine activities. It includes advice on hot work and on permit-to-work systems for those activities identified as high risk.

(e) *Unloading petrol from road tankers*[6] - This gives practical advice and contains a code of practice on regulation 6 with regard to the safe unloading of petrol tankers at petrol filling stations.

5 In addition, the free leaflet *Fire and explosion – How safe is your workplace?*[7] provides a short guide to DSEAR and is aimed at small and medium-sized businesses.

6 Information on DSEAR can also be accessed via HSE's website: www.hse.gov.uk, which is regularly updated.

Regulation 5

Assessment of the risks

Regulation

(1) Where a dangerous substance is or is liable to be present at the workplace, the employer shall make a suitable and sufficient assessment of the risks to his employees which arise from that substance.

(2) The risk assessment shall include consideration of -

(a) the hazardous properties of the substance;

(b) information on safety provided by the supplier, including information contained in any relevant safety data sheet;

(c) the circumstances of the work including -

   (i) the work processes and substances used and their possible interactions;

   (ii) the amount of the substance involved;

   (iii) where the work will involve more than one dangerous substance, the risk presented by such substances in combination; and

   (iv) the arrangements for the safe handling, storage and transport of dangerous substances and of waste containing dangerous substances;

(d) activities, such as maintenance, where there is the potential for a high level of risk;

(e) the effect of measures which have been or will be taken pursuant to these Regulations;

(f) the likelihood that an explosive atmosphere will occur and its persistence;

(g) the likelihood that ignition sources, including electrostatic discharges, will be present and become active and effective;

(h) the scale of the anticipated effects of a fire or an explosion;

(i) any places which are or can be connected via openings to places in which explosive atmospheres may occur; and

(j) such additional safety information as the employer may need in order to complete the risk assessment.

Guidance

Risk assessment

7 To meet the requirements of regulation 5(1) and 5(2), employers will need to carry out a risk assessment before bringing into use any plant, equipment or area which handles, produces or processes dangerous substances or is liable to do so. This needs to be done before making any modifications to that plant, equipment or area and before changing the operating conditions or the type of dangerous substance handled.

ACOP

Changing processes and equipment

8 When considering hazards arising from the design of plant,

ACOP

equipment and workplaces where dangerous substances may be present, the purpose of the risk assessment is to determine measures that will:

(a) avoid or minimise the potential risk of spillage or release of a dangerous substance;

(b) avoid the occurrence of explosive atmospheres both within and outside of the plant and equipment;

(c) prevent plant and equipment from unintentionally igniting dangerous substances and explosive atmospheres;

(d) prevent unintentional or uncontrolled hazardous chemical reactions or decompositions of dangerous substances;

(e) avoid the spread of fires or explosions through interconnected plant and equipment and in work areas; and

(f) mitigate the dangerous effects where a fire or explosion may occur so as not to endanger people.

Guidance

9 When making any change to processes and equipment involving dangerous substances it is important to assess the effects of that change on the safe operating conditions already established for the process or equipment. For most significant changes it will be obvious that there are consequences for safety and that a reassessment is necessary but relatively minor changes can also lead to unsafe working conditions if they are overlooked. For example, changing the supplier of a coating material that is applied to objects and then dried in a heated oven might be overlooked as requiring a reassessment. The new raw material, however, while providing the same colour effect may contain a different or higher level of solvent. This could alter the amount of vapours released into the oven raising the concentration from below the lower explosion limit (LEL) to within the explosion range creating a hazardous situation.

Regulation 6

Elimination or reduction of risks from dangerous substances

Regulation

(1) Every employer shall ensure that risk is either eliminated or reduced so far as is reasonably practicable.

(2) In complying with his duty under paragraph (1), substitution shall by preference be undertaken, whereby the employer shall avoid, so far as is reasonably practicable, the presence or use of a dangerous substance at the workplace by replacing it with a substance or process which either eliminates or reduces the risk.

(3) Where it is not reasonably practicable to eliminate risk pursuant to paragraphs (1) and (2), the employer shall, so far as is reasonably practicable, apply measures, consistent with the risk assessment and appropriate to the nature of the activity or operation -

(a) to control risks, including the measures specified in paragraph (4); and

(b) to mitigate the detrimental effects of a fire or explosion or the other harmful physical effects arising from dangerous substances, including the measures specified in paragraph (5).

Regulation

(4) *The following measures are, in order of priority, those specified for the purposes of paragraph (3)(a) -*

(a) *the reduction of the quantity of dangerous substances to a minimum;*

(b) *the avoidance or minimising of the release of a dangerous substance;*

(c) *the control of the release of a dangerous substance at source;*

(d) *the prevention of the formation of an explosive atmosphere, including the application of appropriate ventilation;*

(e) *ensuring that any release of a dangerous substance which may give rise to risk is suitably collected, safely contained, removed to a safe place, or otherwise rendered safe, as appropriate;*

(f) *the avoidance of -*

  (i) *ignition sources including electrostatic discharges; and*

  (ii) *adverse conditions which could cause dangerous substances to give rise to harmful physical effects; and*

(g) *the segregation of incompatible dangerous substances.*

(5) *The following measures are those specified for the purposes of paragraph (3)(b) -*

(a) *the reduction to a minimum of the number of employees exposed;*

(b) *the avoidance of the propagation of fires or explosions;*

(c) *the provision of explosion pressure relief arrangements;*

(d) *the provision of explosion suppression equipment;*

(e) *the provision of plant which is constructed so as to withstand the pressure likely to be produced by an explosion; and*

(f) *the provision of suitable personal protective equipment.*

(6) *The employer shall arrange for the safe handling, storage and transport of dangerous substances and waste containing dangerous substances.*

(7) *The employer shall ensure that any conditions necessary pursuant to these Regulations for ensuring the elimination or reduction of risk are maintained.*

(8) *The employer shall, so far as is reasonably practicable, take the general safety measures specified in Schedule 1, subject to those measures being consistent with the risk assessment and appropriate to the nature of the activity or operation.*

6

Schedule 1

Schedule 1

General safety measures

1. *The following measures are those specified for the purposes of regulation 6(8).*

Workplace and work processes

2. *Ensuring that the workplace is designed, constructed and maintained so as to reduce risk.*

3. *Designing, constructing, assembling, installing, providing and using suitable work processes so as to reduce risk.*

4. *Maintaining work processes in an efficient state, in efficient working order and in good repair.*

5. *Ensuring that equipment and protective systems meet the following requirements –*

   (a) where power failure can give rise to the spread of additional risk, equipment and protective systems must be able to be maintained in a safe state of operation independently of the rest of the plant in the event of power failure;

   (b) means for manual override must be possible, operated by employees competent to do so, for shutting down equipment and protective systems incorporated within automatic processes which deviate from the intended operating conditions, provided that the provision or use of such means does not compromise safety;

   (c) on operation of emergency shutdown, accumulated energy must be dissipated as quickly and as safely as possible or isolated so that it no longer constitutes a hazard; and

   (d) necessary measures must be taken to prevent confusion between connecting devices.

Organisational measures

6. *The application of appropriate systems of work including –*

   (a) the issuing of written instructions for the carrying out of the work; and

   (b) a system of permits to work with such permits being issued by a person with responsibility for this function prior to the commencement of the work concerned,

where the work is carried out in hazardous places or involves hazardous activities.

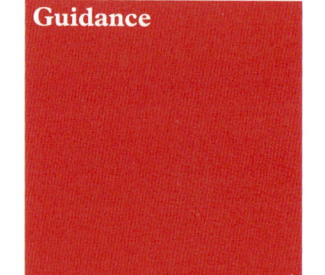

Guidance

General principles on the selection of equipment, etc where dangerous substances are present

10 To meet the requirements of regulation 6 and Schedule 1, employers must take account of the design and organisation of systems of work at the workplace and the provision of suitable work equipment.

11 Employers must ensure that plant, equipment and workplaces are designed, constructed, installed, operated and maintained to reduce the risks arising from dangerous substances. The plant and equipment selected should be suitable for its intended purpose and for the location in which it is to be used.

Guidance

Supply of equipment and protective systems

12   As well as taking into account the requirements of DSEAR, employers must also take into account the requirements of the Provision and Use of Work Equipment Regulations 1998 (PUWER).[8] In addition to containing general requirements relating to the provision and use of work equipment, PUWER requires protection against specific hazards including those of fire and explosion. Detailed guidance and ACOP requirements for PUWER are available in *Safe use of work equipment*.[9]

13   A number of pieces of legislation are derived from European Directives that place duties on suppliers of equipment and also protective systems and devices to ensure that they are safe for their intended use. These regulations contain essential health and safety requirements (EHSRs) that have to be met before the equipment can be placed on the market. Suppliers will demonstrate compliance either by direct comparison with the requirements and by maintaining a technical file or by designing and constructing their equipment to appropriate European harmonised standards. Verification of the compliance may require third party assessment by a notified body. Relevant regulations include:

(a)   the Pressure Equipment Regulations 1999;[10]

(b)   the Equipment and Protective Systems Intended for Use in Potentially Explosive Atmospheres Regulations 1996 (as amended) (EPS);[11] and

(c)   the Supply of Machinery (Safety) Regulations 1992 (as amended).[12]

14   Equipment that has been shown to meet the essential health and safety requirements of a European Directive (or the corresponding national legislation) will carry the CE mark. Equipment intended for use in potentially explosive atmospheres that has been shown to meet the EHSRs of EPS Regulations[11] will carry the explosion protection symbol 'Ex' in a hexagon. Such equipment will also be marked with other relevant safety information, including the equipment group and category, whether it is for use in gas or dust atmospheres and the temperature rating. Further information can be found in Schedule 3 to DSEAR.[1]

15   The above Regulations require equipment suppliers to provide documentation, specifying details of the intended and safe use of that equipment. The documentation may also specify applications for which the equipment is not suitable. For simple applications or simple items of equipment, this documentation may be sufficient to allow the user to select appropriate and safe equipment. For more complex applications, or complex equipment, discussion between the supplier and the user will be necessary before equipment is selected or brought into service.

Guidance

16 It is the duty of employers to consider how and where a piece of equipment is to be installed and to select equipment that is suitable for its intended use (guidance to PUWER[8] regulation 4 also refers to the environment in which it should be considered). Employers will need to take into account:

(a) the substances that may be used with or near to the equipment;

(b) how different substances may react or contribute to a fire or explosion hazard;

(c) where hazardous areas may arise;

(d) how fire or explosion hazards may develop from interconnected plant and process areas; and

(e) instructions provided with the equipment by the supplier.

17 Where an employer selects equipment entirely on the basis of advice from the supplier, under DSEAR[1] and PUWER,[8] the employer still has a responsibility for the safety of that equipment. The supplier will also carry some responsibility under the supply legislation if equipment is later shown to be unsafe.

18 Having decided on the application of the equipment the employer needs to understand which set of supply legislation is relevant and then select equipment that has been shown to meet all the relevant requirements of that legislation. Often more than one European Directive may apply to equipment but the CE mark may only relate to one set of requirements. The CE mark on its own is not sufficient to indicate that the equipment is suitable for its intended purpose and whether all the relevant essential health and safety requirements have been met. It is necessary to read the documentation supplied with the equipment.

19 The following standards provide guidelines on the design and construction of equipment, protective systems and components to achieve adequate fire and explosion prevention and protection:

Safety of machinery – Fire prevention and protection;[13]

Explosive atmospheres – Explosion prevention and protection Part 1 Basic concepts.[14]

20 More detailed standards are available for specific types of equipment and new or revised standards are published regularly.

21 Equipment designed and built by employers for use by their own employees will have to meet the relevant essential health and safety requirements when first brought into use in the same way that any equipment has to when purchased from a supplier or other third party.

22 Where there are no relevant national or international standards available, employers will need to ensure that the equipment is safe by considering the relevant essential health and safety requirements in EPS and by implementing, where applicable, the control measures set out below.

Guidance

Control measures

23   Where a work activity involves a dangerous substance, regulation 6 requires employers to eliminate risks, preferably by substituting the dangerous substance with one that is not dangerous. However, in many cases the nature of the business or activity means that substitution is not possible. In these circumstances employers must reduce risks, so far as is reasonably practicable, by applying the measures in regulations 6(3) and 6(4).

24   Employers must implement the control measures identified by the risk assessment and also, where relevant, the measures detailed below.

ACOP

Reducing the quantity of dangerous substances to a minimum

25   Employers should ensure that the quantity of any dangerous substance stored or processed in plant and equipment at any one time in any workplace is as small as is reasonably practicable having regard to the processes and operations being carried on.

Guidance

26   The extent of any harmful effects from fires or explosions are directly related to the quantity of dangerous substance involved. Employers should seek to minimise the quantity of materials contained or processed at any one time by selecting plant and equipment with the smallest capacity consistent with operational needs. When deciding on the capacity of the plant, the employer should consider the overall risks of an operation and take into account the associated material handling procedures. Product transfer, for example, can give rise to hazardous operations and the overall risks may be lower by selecting increased plant capacity and reducing the number of transfer operations.

27   The hazards of dangerous substances in chemical reactors may be reduced in some cases, by reducing the instantaneous reaction inventory. This may be done, for example, by replacing batch with semi-batch processes, or by process intensification.

ACOP

28   Plant and equipment should be designed, installed and operated to prevent the unintentional accumulation or build up of dangerous substances and their flammable residues.

Guidance

29   Ducts, trunks and casings should be designed and installed to minimise the likelihood of dangerous substances accumulating and giving rise to the risk of fire; for example as a consequence of vapours from dangerous substances condensing out or the deposition of any solid residues. Ductwork used for flammable dusts should be designed, where reasonably practicable, to maintain adequate velocity throughout its length and with smooth inner surfaces and large radius bends. Where dusts or other residues could accumulate, suitable access points for inspection and cleaning should be provided.

30   Plant and equipment should be designed and operated to minimise their fire loading by preventing the unintentional accumulation of dangerous substances and their flammable or unstable residues. Additionally, residues should be prevented from accumulating on surfaces that attain a temperature which could cause them to catch fire and ignite any explosive atmosphere. For example, cellulose nitrate from solutions containing highly flammable liquids should be prevented from accumulating on surfaces with a temperature greater than 120°C. If allowed to build up it could decompose and ignite any flammable mixtures from the highly flammable liquid.

ACOP

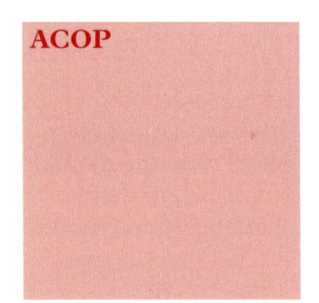

Measures to avoid or minimise the release of a dangerous substance

31 Plant and equipment handling or storing dangerous substances should be designed to prevent any premature loss of contents during its expected life and during foreseeable operating and emergency conditions. The material of construction and any corrosion protection should be able to withstand foreseeable corrosion and abrasion during use and be compatible with any dangerous substances that are produced, used or stored in the plant or equipment.

Guidance

32 Where any plant or equipment operates at a pressure greater than 0.5 bar above atmospheric pressure there are duties on the supplier and user under the Pressure Systems Safety Regulations 2000 (PSSR).[15] These duties are for the user to provide for any person operating the system adequate and suitable instructions for:

(a) the safe operation of the system; and

(b) the action to be taken in the event of any emergency.

33 In addition, the user shall ensure that the pressure system is not operated except in accordance with the instructions provided for the system. The requirements of the PSSR[15] are intended to prevent injury from the hazard of stored energy as a result of the failure of a pressure system or one of its components. However the risk of premature loss of the system's contents will also be minimised if the system is designed, installed and operated in accordance with these Regulations. Detailed guidance and ACOP requirements for the PSSR[15] are available in the publication *Safety of pressure systems*.[16]

ACOP

34 Where reasonably practicable, work processes and operations should be designed to minimise the release of dangerous substances by using pipework, closed vessels and enclosed systems.

35 Plant and equipment should be designed to prevent or minimise the release of dangerous substances into the workroom from any doors, access points and openings provided for charging or removing materials or items.

36 Where the opening of any door, cover, joint or lid on plant or equipment could result in the release of hazardous quantities of dangerous substances into the workroom the plant or equipment should be provided with interlocks, valves or systems of work to prevent such a release.

37 Where in any process or operation any dangerous substance is liable to be spilled or to leak the employer should ensure that, as far as is reasonably practicable, any dangerous substance which is spilt or leaks and can give rise to a hazardous situation is contained or run off to a container or to a safe place, or otherwise treated to make it safe.

Controlling the release of a dangerous substance at source

38 Where dangerous substances may be released into the workroom from access points or openings for charging or removing materials on plant and equipment, adequate local exhaust ventilation should be

ACOP

provided, where reasonably practicable, to prevent or minimise such a release.

39   Where plant, equipment or a process may release dangerous substances that could give rise to explosive atmospheres they should be enclosed, where reasonably practicable, within a cabinet or other suitable enclosure and provided with mechanical ventilation to prevent explosive atmospheres from being released into work areas.

Guidance

40   Plant and equipment designed to the appropriate national or international standard for processing dangerous substances will normally be provided with adequate enclosures and ventilation. Such equipment should be installed in accordance with the manufacturer's instructions and any ventilation ducting routed to a safe place, a recovery unit or a disposal unit.

ACOP

41   Plant and equipment handling or storing dangerous substances should be provided with isolation valves, where reasonably practicable, to minimise leaks after use, to control leaks during use and to enable safe isolation of the plant for maintenance.

42   Where the sudden loss of containment from pipework, pumps and ancillary equipment to storage and process vessels containing dangerous substances could foreseeably give rise to a significant hazard the storage and process vessels should be provided with adequate isolation valves to mitigate the effects of that loss. Where personnel would be exposed to danger when operating the valves manually during an emergency, then the shut-off valves should be remotely operated wherever reasonably practicable.

Guidance

43   The risk assessment carried out in accordance with regulation 5 should be used by employers to decide on the need, location and type of valves necessary for isolating the supply after use, during maintenance and in the event of an emergency.

ACOP

Preventing the formation of an explosive atmosphere

44   Any plant, equipment or process that may release dangerous substances should preferably be located in the open air. Such plant, equipment or process may be provided with suitable weather protection, for example, a canopy designed to prevent the accumulation of dangerous substances. Where it is located indoors, it should, where it is reasonably practicable to do so, be within a suitable adequately ventilated enclosure. Where provision of such an enclosure is not reasonably practicable, the workroom itself should be provided with adequate ventilation, designed to dilute the concentration of foreseeable releases of dangerous substances to a safe level.

45   Plant or equipment should not be located within a workroom or building when it is not possible to maintain the concentration of foreseeable releases of dangerous substances to a safe level.

46   Plant and equipment handling dangerous substances should be designed and operated, where reasonably practicable, to prevent the formation of explosive atmospheres within any enclosed spaces forming part of the plant or equipment and any associated connecting duct work.

Guidance

47 Measures to prevent the formation of explosive atmospheres within plant and equipment include:

(a) control of the release of dangerous substance;

(b) adequate mechanical ventilation;

(c) inerting with a suitable non-reactive gas, such as nitrogen, to maintain oxygen levels below that at which combustion of the dangerous substance can occur; and

(d) maintaining concentration of dangerous substance above the upper explosion limit.

48 Where failure of the control measure could allow an explosive atmosphere to occur appropriate detectors and interlocks should be provided to prevent a hazardous situation arising.

49 Detailed guidance and ACOP requirements on providing adequate ventilation is provided in the DSEAR ACOP on *Control and mitigation measures*.[4]

ACOP

Avoiding ignition sources

50 Employers should ensure, so far as is reasonably practicable, that work equipment cannot unintentionally ignite hazardous concentrations of dangerous substances which may arise either in the workplace or within the equipment itself.

Guidance

51 Detailed guidance and ACOP requirements to control ignition sources are contained in the DSEAR ACOP on *Control and mitigation measures*.[4]

52 Many types of plant are designed for the deliberate combustion of dangerous substances and it is necessary to control the risk of an explosion, which can occur if the plant is not suitably designed and operated. The risk of an explosion can occur with fuels in the form of a gas, vapour, finely divided liquid droplets or finely divided powder. As a minimum, controls are needed to ensure that:

(a) the amount of fuel present at the moment an ignition source is applied will not cause danger;

(b) once combustion has started, fuel is supplied at a controlled rate, and does not accumulate, unburnt, within the equipment;

(c) if flames fail or the combustion process ceases when this is not intended, corrective action is taken before danger can arise; and,

(d) when a plant is shut down, the formation of an explosive atmosphere inside it is prevented.

53 Detailed requirements and design standards have been established for many types of combustion plant. When carrying out a risk assessment, reference should be made to relevant international or national standards or if these are not available to the key safety requirements above.

Guidance

Avoiding adverse conditions that could result in harmful physical effects arising from a dangerous substance

54 Many chemical substances can give rise to harmful physical effects by generating heat and/or generating pressure from released gases and/or vapours following self-reaction, reaction with air or moisture or reaction with other chemical substances. They may also release other flammable or toxic substances.

ACOP

55 Employers should ensure that work processes (including plant and equipment) and workplaces are designed and operated to avoid any adverse conditions that could allow dangerous substances to react or decompose in an uncontrolled manner and give rise to hazardous heat and pressure effects such as the uncontrolled release of other flammable materials.

Guidance

56 Employers should obtain information on the hazards of dangerous substances and identify any adverse conditions that need to be avoided. These could include excessive heat, sunlight, exposure to air or moisture and contact with other incompatible substances.

ACOP

57 Employers should ensure that plant used for chemical reaction processes is designed, constructed, provided with sufficient monitoring and control and operated so as to avoid any adverse conditions that could allow dangerous substances to give rise to hazardous heat and pressure effects such as the uncontrolled release of the plant contents.

Guidance

58 Where it is intended to carry out chemical reactions it will be necessary to carry out a chemical reaction hazard assessment as part of the assessment required by regulation 5. This should provide sufficient information on the reaction kinetics, quantities and rates of heat and any gas generation to allow the plant to be designed safely with the correct process controls and operating conditions. This should include, as necessary:

(a) materials of construction;

(b) vessel design pressure;

(c) agitator configuration and speed;

(d) reactant feed controls;

(e) safe operating temperatures and pressures;

(f) heat transfer and cooling rates;

(g) process instrumentation and interlocks; and

(h) process venting.

59 Both normal operation and the effects of foreseeable process faults should be considered during the safety assessment. Further information on the assessment and control of chemical reaction processes is given in *Designing and operating safe chemical reaction processes*.[17]

ACOP

Mitigation measures

60 Where a work activity involves a dangerous substance and the risks from it cannot be eliminated, regulation 6 requires employers to apply measures to mitigate the detrimental effects of a fire or explosion or other harmful physical effects arising from dangerous substances (including mixtures of dangerous substances) which are appropriate to the nature of the activity and are consistent with the assessment required by regulation 5.

Guidance

61 Having provided the appropriate control measures employers should still consider, as part of their overall risk assessment, the residual risk of a fire or explosion occurring and take reasonably practicable measures to mitigate the detrimental effects arising from that risk.

ACOP

Reducing to a minimum the number of people exposed

62 Workplaces in which the quantity of dangerous substance manufactured, used or manipulated would have particular influence on the scale or nature of any incident involving fire or explosion, should be adequately separated from other parts of the premises and the site boundary.

63 Workrooms within buildings containing such workplaces should be separated from the rest of the building by physical barriers that are fire-resisting structures. Workplaces should also be adequately separated from areas where the dangerous substances are stored.

Guidance

64 Dangerous substances that give rise to a significant risk of fire during handling or processing include those classified under the Chemicals (Hazard Information and Packaging for Supply) Regulations 2002 (CHIP)[18] as explosive, oxidising, extremely flammable, highly flammable and flammable. However, some of the substances classified as flammable that have a high flashpoint may not give rise to a significant risk of fire unless processed at high pressure or at temperatures above their flashpoint. A detailed risk assessment for these substances on the way they are used or handled may indicate that fire-resisting requirements can be relaxed to some degree.

65 Detailed guidance and ACOP requirements on providing adequate separation and fire-resisting structures is provided in the DSEAR ACOP on *Control and mitigation measures*.[4]

66 Control rooms and other occupied buildings on sites processing or handling significant quantities of dangerous substances should be positioned or designed to provide protection from potential fires, explosions and ingress of dangerous substances. Additional guidance on protecting buildings for chemical plant is contained in *Guidance for the location and design of occupied buildings on chemical manufacturing sites*.[19]

ACOP

Measures to avoid the propagation of fires or explosions from plant and equipment

67 Plant and equipment processing dangerous substances that can give rise to hazardous explosive atmospheres should be designed and installed with measures that prevent fire and explosion from spreading to other vulnerable equipment or into the workroom.

Guidance

68   Mitigation measures for plant and equipment processing highly flammable solids and dusts include rotary valves, explosion suppression barriers, fast acting valves, chokes and baffles. Mitigation measures for interconnected plant and equipment processing flammable gases and vapours include flame arresters, fast acting valves and suppression barriers.

69   Vent pipes from plant containing flammable, highly flammable or extremely flammable liquids, required for normal operation, should discharge to a safe place outside and normally be provided with a flame arrestor.

ACOP

70   **Means should be provided to prevent or reduce the likelihood of failure of plant containing a dangerous substance as result of over-pressurisation and/or weakening due to exposure to heat, including fire, where such failure may lead to harm.**

Guidance

71   Means to prevent and reduce failure include the provision of suitable pressure relieving devices, such as pressure and hydrostatic relief valves; and measures for mitigating the effects of fire, such as water deluge systems and passive fire protection coatings. Further guidance and ACOP requirements relating to other fire protection matters are detailed in the main DSEAR[1] guidance document.

ACOP

72   **Dryers, ovens, cabinets, and other enclosures in which flammable concentrations of dangerous substances may reasonably be expected to be released, and any connecting ducts, trunks and casings used for ventilation from these items of plant, should be fire-resisting structures.**

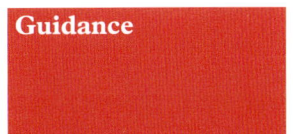

Guidance

73   The fire-resisting requirements for these structures are detailed in the DSEAR ACOP on *Control and mitigation measures*.[4]

74   The assessment required by regulation 5 should consider the need for suitable pressure relieving devices and appropriate fire protection and take into account foreseeable events including:

(a)   fires involving releases of dangerous substances from that or other plant;

(b)   other fires on site or at the boundary not involving a dangerous substance;

(c)   sudden warming of cryogenic substances as a result of normal and abnormal operating conditions or following changes in atmospheric conditions; and

(d)   thermal expansion of enclosed or trapped liquids caused by atmospheric warming or fire.

75   A prolonged external fire at an enclosed vessel will cause an over-pressure as the gases or vapours increase in temperature. At the same time, the effects of the heat will be to reduce the structural integrity of the vessel that could result in its catastrophic failure with the sudden release and ignition of its contents. The assessment should consider the consequences of the unlikely but extremely hazardous event of catastrophic containment failure.

ACOP

Measures to mitigate the effects of an explosion (including explosion relief, suppression and pressure resistant plant)

76   **Where there is a residual risk that an explosion could occur and cause injury, employers must ensure plant and equipment is provided with explosion protection measures to minimise that risk of injury.**

Guidance

77 Explosion protection measures for plant and equipment processing dangerous substances include explosion relief venting, explosion suppression equipment, pressure shock resistant plant and pressure resistant plant. The design of the protection measure should mitigate possible explosions by:

(a) relieving the explosion pressures and/or hot gases to a safe place outside of the workroom;

(b) suppressing the explosion before dangerous pressures build-up; and

(c) safely containing the explosion without the plant rupturing.

78 Plant and equipment normally requiring explosion protection or emergency relief venting, include:

(a) ovens and dryers normally operating with concentrations of dangerous substances below 25% of the LEL but without sufficient process control to prevent deviations above 25% LEL;

(b) ovens and dryers operating with concentrations of dangerous substances above 25% of the LEL;

(c) reactors where there is a significant residual risk from the process of a runaway reaction (unless alternative protection measures are provided such as crash cooling, reaction inhibition and quenching);

(d) cyclones, dust filters and other dust handling plant where there is a risk of ignition;

(e) spray dryers producing combustible dusts;

(f) silos storing combustible dusts;

(g) aerosol filling rooms using liquefied flammable gases;

(h) other plant and equipment in which explosive atmospheres may occur and ignition sources cannot be eliminated;

(i) storerooms for highly flammable and extremely flammable liquids; and,

(j) storage of liquid petroleum gas (LPG) and compressed natural gas in buildings.

ACOP

Other issues to consider on the control and mitigation of risks

79 Employers should ensure that measures to eliminate or reduce risks and to mitigate the detrimental effects of a fire or explosion or the other harmful physical effects arising from dangerous substances include the following features and procedures:

(a) the maintenance of plant, equipment and control systems in an efficient state, in efficient working order and in good repair;

(b) the safe handling, storage and transport of dangerous substances and of waste containing dangerous substances; and

(c) the segregation of incompatible dangerous substances.

Guidance

80 Detailed guidance and ACOP requirements for the maintenance of plant and equipment arising from PUWER[8] is available in *Safe use of work equipment*.[9]

81 Guidance and ACOP requirements for the storage of dangerous substances and the segregation of incompatible dangerous substances are detailed in the DSEAR ACOP on *Storage of dangerous substances*.[3]

ACOP

Making redundant plant and equipment safe

82 In order to meet the requirements of regulation 6(6) in relation to the safe handling, storage and transport of dangerous substances, employers must consider the risks arising from the dismantling and disposal of redundant equipment that has been used for work involving dangerous substances.

Guidance

83 Based on the findings of their risk assessment, employers should decide upon and implement appropriate control measures to ensure the safety of employees and others during the cleaning and decommissioning of redundant plant, equipment, buildings and contaminated areas prior to them being taken out of use and their subsequent storage, disposal or demolition.

ACOP

General requirements

84 Redundant plant and equipment which has been used for storing, transporting, handling or treating dangerous substances should be made safe before being mothballed, dismantled, transferred to a holding area or removed from site.

Guidance

85 The plant and equipment should first be adequately isolated from sources of dangerous substances (eg by permanent disconnection or by use of blanking plates) and drained or cleaned of residual material. Additional cleaning or inerting may be required depending on the risk assessment and the proposed method of disposal. Normally the plant and equipment should be effectively cleaned of all residues and where necessary gas freed before being mothballed, dismantled, transferred to a holding area or removed from site. The DSEAR ACOP on *Safe maintenance, repair and cleaning procedures*[5] provides further information and guidance on dismantling and decommissioning plant and equipment.

86 Where plant or equipment containing residual product is to be removed from site without cleaning or gas freeing it is necessary to ensure that it can be handled and transported safely and that those receiving it are aware of the hazards and are competent to deal with them. The employer should ensure that the risk assessment identifies the hazards and the necessary control measures for the disposal procedures and that, where available, agreed industry standards are followed.

ACOP

Disposal of static vessels containing LPG

87 Redundant bulk LPG vessels with a capacity of greater than 30 cubic metres should be emptied and gas freed before being removed from site. LPG vessels with a capacity of between 5 and 30 cubic metres should have any liquid product removed and the pressure inside the vessel reduced to less than 1 bar before they are removed from site. LPG vessels with a capacity of less than 5 cubic metres should only be removed from a site when any liquid material remaining has been

ACOP

reduced to the minimum practicable amount. LPG cylinders (transportable pressure receptacles) for which there is no further use should be returned to the supplier.

Guidance

88 Guidance on removing redundant bulk LPG vessels from sites is contained in the LPG Association Code of Practice No 26 - *Uplifting of static LPG vessels from sites and their carriage to and from site by road*.[20] The minimum practicable amount of LPG that can remain in a vessel of less than five cubic metres when it is removed from site is 50 kg.

ACOP

Disposal of underground petrol tanks

89 Redundant underground petrol tanks should be made permanently safe by completely filling with a suitable solid material or by removing them from site. Where tanks are to be excavated they should be isolated from all sources of petrol and either cleaned and gas-freed or made temporarily safe with a suitable inert foam or gas. Where tanks, which have been made temporarily safe, are to be taken off site for cleaning and disposal they should be maintained in a safe condition prior to and during transport and subsequent demolition.

Guidance

90 Suitable solid materials for filling underground storage tanks in situ include sand/cement slurry, foamed concrete and urea amino plastic foam. Prior to adding the solid material the tank should be emptied of residual product and then made safe by filling with an inert material such as nitrogen foam, nitrogen gas, water, carbon dioxide or combustion gas. Alternatively the tank can be made safe prior to filling by cleaning and degassing methods.

References and further reading

References

1 *The Dangerous Substances and Explosive Atmospheres Regulations 2002* SI 2002/2776 The Stationery Office 2002 ISBN 0 11 042957 5

2 *Dangerous Substances and Explosive Atmospheres. Dangerous Substances and Explosive Atmospheres Regulations. Approved Code of Practice and guidance* L138 HSE Books 2003 ISBN 0 7176 2203 7

3 *Storage of dangerous substances. Dangerous Substances and Explosive Atmospheres Regulations 2002. Approved Code of Practice and guidance* L135 HSE Books 2003 ISBN 0 7176 2200 2

4 *Control and mitigation measures. Dangerous Substances and Explosive Atmospheres Regulations 2002. Approved Code of Practice and guidance* L136 HSE Books 2003 ISBN 0 7176 2201 0

5 *Safe maintenance, repair and cleaning procedures. Dangerous Substances and Explosive Atmospheres Regulations 2002. Approved Code of Practice and guidance* L137 HSE Books 2003 ISBN 0 7176 2202 9

6 *Unloading petrol from road tankers. Dangerous Substances and Explosive Atmospheres Regulations 2002. Approved Code of Practice and guidance* L133 HSE Books 2003 ISBN 0 7176 2197 9

7 *Fire and explosion: How safe is your workplace? A short guide to the Dangerous Substances and Explosive Atmospheres Regulations* Leaflet INDG370 HSE Books 2002 (single copy free or priced packs of 5 ISBN 0 7176 2589 3)

8 *The Provision and Use of Work Equipment Regulations 1998* SI 1998/2306 The Stationery Office 1998 ISBN 0 11 079599 7

9 *Safe use of work equipment. Provision and Use of Work Equipment Regulations 1998. Approved Code of Practice and guidance* L22 (Second edition) HSE Books 1998 ISBN 0 7176 1626 6

10 *The Pressure Equipment Regulations 1999* SI 1999/2001 The Stationery Office 1999 ISBN 0 11 082790 2

11 *The Equipment and Protective Systems Intended for Use in Potentially Explosive Atmospheres 1996* SI 1996/192 The Stationery Office 1996 ISBN 0 11 053999 0

12 *The Supply of Machinery (Safety) Regulations 1992* SI 1992/3073 The Stationery Office 1992 ISBN 0 11 025719 7

13 *Safety of machinery. Fire prevention and protection* BS EN 13478:2002 British Standards Institute 2002

14 *Explosive Atmospheres. Explosion prevention and protection. Part 1 Basic concepts and methodology* BS EN 1127-1:1998 British Standards Institute 1998

15 *The Pressure Systems Safety Regulations 2000* SI 2000/128 The Stationery Office 2000 ISBN 0 11 085836 0

16 *Safety of pressure systems. Pressure Systems Safety Regulations 2000. Approved Code of Practice* L122 HSE Books 2000 ISBN 0 7176 1767 X

17   *Designing and operating safe chemical reaction processes* HSG143 HSE Books 2000 ISBN 0 7176 1051 9

18   *The Chemicals (Hazard Information and Packaging for Supply) Regulations 2002* SI 2002/1689 The Stationery Office 2002 ISBN 0 11 042419 0

19   *Guidance for the location and design of occupied buildings on chemical manufacturing sites* Chemical Industries Association 1998 ISBN 1 85897 077 6

20   *Uplifting of static LPG vessels from site and their carriage to and from site by road* Code of Practice 26 LP Gas Association 1999 available from LP Gas Association, Pavilion 16, Headlands Business Park, Salisbury Road, Ringwood, Hampshire BH24 3PB, Fax 01425 471131

Further reading

Guidelines on the application of Directive 94/9/EC of 23 March 1994 on the approximation of the laws of the Member States concerning equipment and protective systems for use in potentially explosive atmospheres available online at http://europa.eu.int/comm/enterprise/atex/index.htm

Safe handling of combustible dusts: Precautions against explosions HSG103 HSE Books 2003 ISBN 0 7176 2726 8

Safe use and handling of flammable liquids HSG140 HSE Books 1996 ISBN 0 7176 0967 7

The storage of flammable liquids in tanks HSG176 HSE Books 1998 ISBN 0 7176 1470 0

The storage of flammable liquids in containers HSG51 (Second edition) HSE Books 1998 ISBN 0 7176 1471 9

Designing and operating safe chemical reaction processes HSG143 HSE Books 2000 ISBN 0 7176 1051 9

The Dangerous Substances and Explosive Atmospheres Regulations 2002. A short guide for the offshore industry HSE Offshore Division Operations Notice 58 available online at http://www.hse.gov.uk/hid/osd/notices/on_index.htm

The Equipment and Protective Systems Intended for use in Potentially Explosive Atmospheres Regulations 1996. A short guide for the offshore industry HSE Offshore Division Operations Notice 59 available online at http://www.hse.gov.uk/hid/osd/notices/on_index.htm

A guide to the integrity, workplace environment and miscellaneous aspects of the Offshore Installations and Wells (Design and Construction etc) Regulations 1996. Guidance on Regulations L85 HSE Books 1996 ISBN 0 7176 1164 7

The safe isolation of plant and equipment HSE Books 1997 ISBN 0 7176 0871 9

Flame arresters: Preventing the spread of fires and explosions in equipment that contains flammable gases and vapours HSG158 HSE Books 1996 ISBN 0 7176 1191 4

The spraying of flammable liquids HSG178 HSE Books 1998 ISBN 0 7176 1483 2

Control of safety risks at gas turbines used for power generation PM84 HSE Books 2000 ISBN 0 71716 1808 0